How Does the Mail Work?

by
Kristin Cashore

PEARSON

Scott
Foresman

Editorial Offices: Glenview, Illinois • Parsippany, New Jersey • New York, New York
Sales Offices: Needham, Massachusetts • Duluth, Georgia • Glenview, Illinois
Coppell, Texas • Ontario, California • Mesa, Arizona

I will show you how the mail works.
First, I write a letter to my aunt in a faraway town. I write about school. I draw a picture of me, my parents, and my dog.

Auntie Joan
56 River Street
Anytown, NY 10108

I put the letter in an envelope and
seal it. I write my aunt's address on the
envelope in my best handwriting.

Then I put a stamp on the envelope. I make sure it sticks. I don't want it to wash away.

I go to the mailbox near my home. My dog keeps me company. I open the box and drop the letter in.

A mail carrier empties the mailbox. He brings the mail to a post office. It is sorted and put on a truck. Then it goes to all parts of the country.

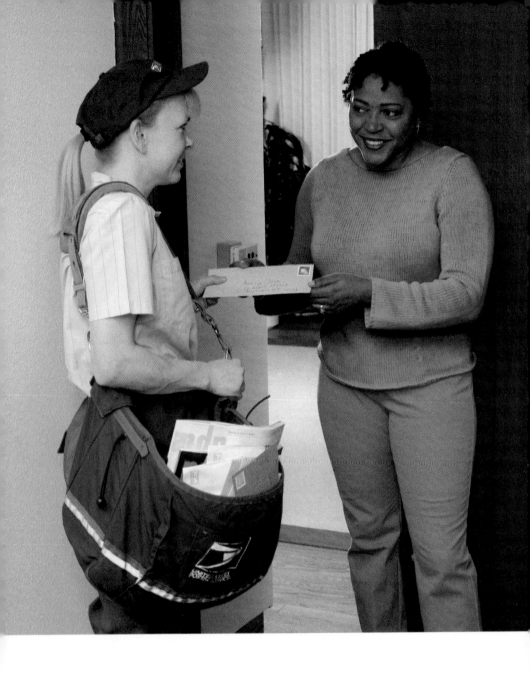

Mail carriers deliver the letters, even if it's raining or cold. The mail carriers put the letters in the right mailboxes.

At last, my aunt gets my letter! She is so happy. I hope I get an answer soon!